CROSS
EXAMINATION

Resources by Lee Strobel

The Case for Christ

The Case for Christ audio

The Case for Christ—Student Edition (with Jane Vogel)

The Case for Christmas

The Case for Christmas audio

The Case for a Creator

The Case for a Creator audio

The Case for Creator—Student Edition (with Jane Vogel)

The Case for Easter

The Case for Faith

The Case for Faith audio

The Case for Faith—Student Edition (with Jane Vogel)

The Case for the Real Jesus

The Case for the Real Jesus audio

Discussing the Da Vinci Code curriculum
(with Garry Poole)

Discussing the Da Vinci Code discussion guide
(with Garry Poole)

Experiencing the Passion of Jesus (with Garry Poole)

Exploring the Da Vinci Code (with Garry Poole)

Faith Under Fire curriculum series

God's Outrageous Claims

Inside the Mind of Unchurched Harry and Mary

Off My Case for Kids

Surviving a Spiritual Mismatch in Marriage
(with Leslie Strobel)

Surviving a Spiritual Mismatch in Marriage audio

What Jesus Would Say

LEE STROBEL

CROSS EXAMINATION

Investigating The Evidence For Jesus

ZONDERVAN.com/
AUTHORTRACKER
follow your favorite authors

ZONDERVAN®

Cross Examination
Copyright © 1998, 2006 by Lee Strobel

Excerpted from *The Case for Christ* © 1998 by Lee Strobel and
published by Zondervan

Requests for information should be addressed to:

Zondervan, *Grand Rapids, Michigan 49530*

ISBN 978-0-310-61007-6

Printed in the United States of America

08 09 10 • 18 17 16 15 14 13 12 11 10 9 8 7 6 5 4 3 2

CONTENTS

INTRODUCTION

My friends and I were celebrating at an Italian restaurant across the street from the University of Missouri. I was set to graduate in a few days, and I had just accepted a job offer: a three-month internship at the *Chicago Tribune*, with a promise that if I performed well, I'd get a permanent job as a reporter.

At one point during the meal, somewhere between the breadsticks and the Neapolitan ice cream, my best friend, Ersin, made an offhand remark about how my internship was certainly a great gift from God.

His comment startled me. During the four years I'd known Ersin, I don't think we'd ever talked about religion.

"Wait a minute, let me get this straight," I said. "Are you telling me that someone as intelligent as you — valedictorian, science whiz, and all that — that you actually believe that God exists? I always figured you were beyond that!"

It was clear that Ersin was equally surprised. "What are you trying to tell me?" he said. "Are you saying there isn't a God? Are you telling me that someone as intelligent as you doesn't believe in God? You've got to be kidding!"

We were both genuinely astonished. I couldn't believe that a sharp person like Ersin had actually bought into a fairy tale like the existence of an all-powerful, all-knowing Creator of the universe. Hadn't he learned anything at college?

If you could freeze-frame my attitude toward God, that would be it: Intelligent people didn't believe in him. All it took was a quick look at the evidence to know that Christianity was nothing but superstition and wishful thinking.

But to be honest, that's all I had ever really given the evidence: a quick look. And I was happy to keep it that way for years — until one day, my life took a strange turn, pushing me into an all-out investigation into the facts surrounding the case for Christianity.

That's what this book is about. I'll take you along as I retrace the events that led to a nearly 2-year exploration of the evidence for and against believing in Christ.

After weighing the evidence, I made my decision. But I can't make yours. That's your choice. I hope you take it seriously, because there may be more at stake than just idle curiosity. If Jesus is to be believed — and I realize that may be a big if for you at this point — then nothing is more important than how you respond to him.

Check out the evidence for yourself.

1

THE IDENTITY EVIDENCE

Was Jesus Really Convinced That He Was the Son of God?

John Douglas has an uncanny ability to look into the minds of people he has never met.

As the original "psychological profiler" for the Federal Bureau of Investigation, Douglas would gather information at a crime scene and then use his insights to peer inside the personality of the still-at-large perpetrator.

Case in point: Douglas predicted that the "Trailside Killer," a serial murderer who stalked wooded areas near San Francisco from 1979 to 1981, would be someone who had a speech impediment as well as tendencies toward animal cruelty, bed-wetting, and arson. Sure enough, the person finally arrested and convicted in the case fit those descriptions perfectly.[1]

With a doctorate in psychology, years of experience as a detective, and a natural talent for understanding human behavior, Douglas has become renowned for his profiling prowess. He has coauthored several bestsellers on the topic, and when Jodie Foster won the Oscar for her performance in *Silence of the Lambs*, she publicly thanked Douglas for being the real-life figure behind her character's FBI mentor.

How is Douglas able to understand the thinking process of individuals he has never even talked to? "Behavior reflects personality," Douglas explained to *Biography* magazine.[2]

In other words, Douglas closely examines the evidence left behind at the crime scene and, where possible, interviews victims to find out exactly what the criminal said and did. From these clues — the left-behind products of the person's behavior — he deduces the individual's psychological makeup.

Now to Jesus: without dialoguing with him, how can we possibly delve into his mind to determine what his motivations, intentions, and self-understanding were? How do we know who he thought he was and what he understood his mission to be?

By looking at his behavior, Douglas would say. If we want to figure out whether Jesus thought he was the Messiah or Son of God — or merely considered himself to be a rabbi or prophet — we need to look at what he did, what he said, and how he related to others.

The question of what Jesus thought about himself is a critical issue. Some professors maintain that the myth of Jesus' deity was superimposed on the Jesus tradition by overzealous supporters years after his death. The real Jesus, these professors believe, would roll over in his grave if he knew people were worshiping him. If you strip away the legends and go back to the earliest material about him, they say you'll find he never aspired to be anything more than an itinerant teacher and occasional rabble-rouser.

But is the evidence of history on their side? To find out, I flew to Lexington, Kentucky, and drove the winding roads past a series of picturesque horse farms to track down the scholar whose acclaimed book *The Christology of Jesus* confronts this very subject.

INTERVIEW:
BEN WITHERINGTON III, PH.D.

There isn't much to tiny Wilmore, Kentucky, except Asbury Theological Seminary, where I found

Ben Witherington's office on the fourth floor of a colonial-style building off the rustic community's main drag. With the gracious hospitality of a Southern gentleman, the North Carolina native offered me a comfortable chair and some coffee as we sat down to discuss who Jesus of Nazareth thought he was.

"The truth is that Jesus was a bit mysterious about his identity, wasn't he?" I asked as Witherington pulled up a chair across from me. "He tended to shy away from forthrightly proclaiming himself to be the Messiah or Son of God. Was that because he didn't think of himself in those terms or because he had other reasons?"

"No, it's not because he didn't think of himself in those terms," Witherington said as he settled into his chair and crossed his legs. "If he had simply announced, 'Hi, folks; I'm God,' that would have been heard as 'I'm Yahweh,' because the Jews of his day didn't have any concept of the Trinity. They only knew of God the Father — whom they called Yahweh — and not God the Son or God the Holy Spirit.

"So if someone were to say he was God, that wouldn't have made any sense to them and would have been seen as clear-cut blasphemy. And it would have been counterproductive to Jesus in his efforts to get people to listen to his message.

"Besides, there were already a host of expectations about what the Messiah would look like, and Jesus didn't want to be pigeonholed into somebody else's categories. Consequently, he was very careful about what he said publicly. In private with his disciples — that was a different story, but the gospels primarily tell us about what he did in public."

EXPLORING THE EARLIEST TRADITIONS

"What clues can we find about Jesus' self-understanding from the way he related to others?"

Witherington thought for a moment, then replied, "Look at his relationship with his disciples. Jesus has twelve disciples, yet notice that he's not one of the Twelve."

While that may sound like a detail without a difference, Witherington said it's quite significant.

"If the Twelve represent a renewed Israel, where does Jesus fit in?" he asked. "He's not just part of Israel, not merely part of the redeemed group, he's forming the group — just as God in the Old Testament formed his people and set up the twelve tribes of Israel. That's a clue about what Jesus thought of himself."

Witherington went on to describe a clue that can be found in Jesus' relationship with John the Baptist. "Jesus says, 'Of all people born of woman, John is the greatest man on earth.' Having said that, he then goes even further in his ministry than the Baptist did — by doing miracles, for example. What does that say about what he thinks of himself?

"And his relationship with the religious leaders is perhaps the most revealing. Jesus makes the truly radical statement that it's not what enters a person that defiles him but what comes out of his heart. Frankly, this sets aside huge portions of the Old Testament book of Leviticus, with its meticulous rules concerning purity.

"Now, the Pharisees didn't like this message. They wanted to keep things as they were, but Jesus said, 'No, God has further plans. He's doing a new thing.' We have to ask, What kind of person thinks he has the authority to set aside the divinely inspired Jewish Scriptures and supplant them with his own teaching?

"And what about his relationship — if we can call it that — with the Roman authorities? We have to ask why they crucified him. If he had merely been an innocuous sage telling nice little parables, how did he end up on a cross, especially at a Passover season, when no Jew wants any Jew to be executed? There had to be a reason why the sign above his head said, 'This is the King of the Jews.' "

Witherington let that last comment hang in the air, before providing the explanation himself: "Either Jesus had made that verbal claim," he said, "or someone clearly thought he did."

BY THE FINGER OF GOD

While Jesus' relationships provide one window into his self-understanding, Witherington said that Jesus' deeds — especially his miracles — offer additional insights. However, I raised my hand to stop him.

"Certainly you can't say that Jesus' miracles establish that he thought he was God," I said, "since later his own disciples went out and did the same things — and certainly they weren't making claims of deity."

"No, it's not the fact that Jesus did miracles that illuminates his self-understanding," replied Witherington. "What's important is how he interprets his miracles."

"What do you mean?" I asked.

"Jesus says, 'If I, by the finger of God, cast out demons, then you will know that the kingdom of God has come upon you.' He's not like other miracle workers who do amazing things and then life proceeds as it always has. No — to Jesus, his miracles are a sign indicating the coming of the kingdom of God. They are a foretaste of what the kingdom is going to be like. And that sets Jesus apart."

Again I interrupted. "Elaborate on that a bit," I said. "How does it set him apart?"

"Jesus sees his miracles as bringing about something unprecedented — the coming of God's dominion," replied Witherington. "He doesn't merely see himself as a worker of miracles; he sees himself as the one in whom and through whom the promises of God come to pass. And that's a not-too-thinly-veiled claim of transcendence."

I nodded. Now his point made sense to me. With that I turned to the words of Jesus, in search of more clues concerning his self-understanding.

"He was called Rabbouni, or 'Rabbi,' by his followers," I said. "Doesn't this imply that he merely taught like the other rabbis of his day?"

Witherington grinned. "Actually," he said, "Jesus taught in a radical new way. He begins his teachings with the phrase 'Amen I say to you,' which is to say, 'I swear in advance to the truthfulness of what I'm about to say.' This was absolutely revolutionary."

"How so?" I asked.

He replied, "In Judaism you needed the testimony of two witnesses, so witness A could witness the truth of witness B and vice versa. But Jesus witnesses to the truth of his own sayings. Instead of basing his teaching on the authority of others, he speaks on his own authority.

"So here is someone who considered himself to have authority above and beyond what the Old Testament prophets had. He believed he possessed not only divine inspiration, as King David did, but also divine authority and the power of direct divine utterance."

In addition to employing the "Amen" phrase in his teaching, Jesus used the term "Abba" when he was relating to God. "What does that tell us about what he thought about himself?" I asked.

"'Abba' connotes intimacy in a relationship between a child and his father," Witherington explained. "Interestingly, it's also the term disciples used for a beloved teacher in early Judaism. But Jesus used it of God — and as far as I can tell, he and his followers were the only ones praying to God that way."

When I asked Witherington to expand on the importance of this, he said, "In the context in which

Jesus operated, it was customary for Jews to work around having to say the name of God. His name was the most holy word you could speak, and they even feared mispronouncing it. If they were going to address God, they might say something like, 'The Holy One, blessed be he,' but they were not going to use his personal name."

"And 'Abba' is a personal term," I said.

"Very personal," he replied. "It's the term of endearment in which a child would say to a parent, 'Father Dearest, what would you have me do?' "

However, I spotted an apparent inconsistency. "Wait a second," I interjected. "Praying 'Abba' must not imply that Jesus thinks he's God, because he taught his disciples to use the same term in their own prayers, and they're not God."

"Actually," came Witherington's reply, "the significance of 'Abba' is that Jesus is the initiator of an intimate relationship that was previously unavailable. The question is, What kind of person can change the terms of relating to God? What kind of person can initiate a new covenantal relationship with God?"

His distinction made sense to me. "So how significant do you consider Jesus' use of 'Abba' to be?" I asked.

"Quite significant," he answered. "It implies that Jesus had a degree of intimacy with God that is unlike anything in the Judaism of his day. And listen, here's the kicker: Jesus is saying that only through having a relationship with him does this kind of prayer language — this kind of 'Abba' relationship with God — become possible. That says volumes about how he regarded himself."

At this point I paused to take stock of what Witherington had said. When I put together the clues from Jesus' relationships, miracles, and words, his perception of his identity came into sharp focus.

There seemed little question, based upon the earliest evidence, that Jesus considered himself to be more than a doer of great deeds, more than a teacher, more than another prophet in a line of many. There was ample evidence to conclude that he thought of himself in unique and supreme terms — but exactly how sweeping was this self-understanding?

"Is there any evidence," I asked Witherington, "that Jesus ever had an identity crisis?"

"Not an identity crisis, although I do believe he had points of identity confirmation," the professor replied. "At his baptism, at his temptation, at the Transfiguration, in the Garden of Gethsemane —

these are crisis moments in which God confirmed to him who he was and what his mission was.

"For instance, I don't think it's accidental that his ministry does not begin in earnest until after his baptism, when he hears the voice saying, 'You are my Son, with whom I am well pleased.' "

"What did he think his mission was?"

"He saw his job as coming to free the people of God, so his mission was directed to Israel."

"Specifically to Israel," I stressed.

"Yes, that's correct," Witherington said. "There's very little evidence that he sought out Gentiles during his ministry — that was a mission for the later church. You see, the promises of the prophets had come to Israel — and to Israel he must go."

And what exactly was he? As I was wrapping up my time with Witherington, I wanted him to sum it up for me. Taking all his research into consideration, what was his personal conclusion about who Jesus saw himself to be? I posed the question, sat back, and let him spell it out — which he did, with eloquence and conviction.

"Jesus thought he was the person appointed by God to bring in the climactic saving act of God in human history. He believed he was the agent of God to carry that out — that he had been authorized by

God, empowered by God, he spoke for God, and he was directed by God to do this task. So what Jesus said, God said. What Jesus did was the work of God.

"Under the Jewish concept of agency, 'a man's agent is as himself.' Remember how Jesus sent out his apostles and said, 'Whatever they do to you, they've done to me'? There was a strong connection between a man and his agent whom he sends on a mission.

"Well, Jesus believed he was on a divine mission, and the mission was to redeem the people of God. The implication is that the people of God were lost and that God had to do something — as he had always done — to intervene and set them back on the right track. But there was a difference this time. This was the last time. This was the last chance.

"Did Jesus believe he was the Son of God, the anointed one of God? The answer is yes. Did he see himself as the Son of Man? The answer is yes. Did he see himself as the final Messiah? Yes, that's the way he viewed himself. Did he believe that anybody less than God could save the world? No, I don't believe he did.

"And here's where the paradox gets as quizzical as it can possibly get: the way God was going to save the world was by his Son dying. The most human of all human acts — to die.

"Now, God, in his divine nature, doesn't die. So how was God going to get this done? How was God going to be the Savior of the human race? He had to come as a human being to accomplish that task. And Jesus believed he was the one to do it.

"Jesus said in Mark 10:45, 'I did not come to be served but to serve and give my life as a ransom in place of the many.' This is either the highest form of megalomania or it's the example of somebody who really believes, as he said, 'I and the Father are one.' In other words, 'I have the authority to speak for the Father; I have the power to act for the Father; if you reject me, you've rejected the Father.'

"Even if you eliminated the fourth gospel and just read the synoptics, this would still be the conclusion you would come to. And it is the conclusion that Jesus would have led us to if we had a Bible study and asked him this question.

"We have to ask, Why is there no other first-century Jew who has millions of followers today? Why isn't there a John the Baptist movement? Why, of all first-century figures, including the Roman emperors, is Jesus still worshiped today, while the others have crumbled into the dust of history?

"It's because this Jesus — the historical Jesus — is also the living Lord. That's why. It's because he's still around, while the others are long gone."

2

THE FINGERPRINT EVIDENCE

Did Jesus — and Jesus Alone — Match the Identity of the Messiah?

It was an uneventful Saturday at the Hiller home in Chicago. Clarence Hiller spent the afternoon painting the trim on the outside of his two-story house on West 104th Street. By early evening he and his family had retired to bed. However, what happened next would change criminal law in America forever.

The Hillers woke in the early morning hours of September 19, 1910, and became suspicious that a gaslight near their daughter's bedroom had gone out. Clarence went to investigate. His wife heard a quick succession of sounds: a scuffle, two men tumbling down the stairs, two gunshots, and the slamming of the front door. She emerged to find Clarence dead at the foot of the stairs.

Police arrested Thomas Jennings, a convicted burglar, less than a mile away. There was blood on his clothes and his left arm had been injured — both, he said, from falling on a streetcar. In his pocket they found the same kind of gun that had been used to shoot Clarence Hiller, but they couldn't determine if it was the murder weapon.

Knowing they needed more to convict Jennings, detectives scoured the inside of Hiller's home in a search for additional clues. One fact soon became obvious: the killer had entered through a rear kitchen window. Detectives went outside — and there, next to that window, forever imprinted in the white paint that the murder victim himself had so carefully applied to a railing only hours before his death, they found four clear fingerprints from someone's left hand.

Fingerprint evidence was a new concept at the time, having been recently introduced at an international police exhibition in St. Louis. So far, fingerprints had never been used to convict anyone of murder in the United States.

Despite strong objections by defense attorneys that such evidence was unscientific and inadmissible, four officers testified that the fingerprints in the paint perfectly matched those of Thomas Jennings — and him alone. The jury found Jennings guilty, the Illinois Supreme Court upheld his conviction in a historic ruling, and he was later hanged.[1]

The premise behind fingerprint evidence is simple: each individual has unique ridges on his or her fingers. When a print found on an object matches the pattern of ridges on a person's finger, investigators can conclude with scientific certainty that this specific individual has touched that object.

In many criminal cases, fingerprint identification is the pivotal evidence. I remember covering a trial in which a single thumbprint found on the cellophane wrapper of a cigarette package was the determining factor in convicting a twenty-year-old burglar of murdering a college coed.[2] That's how conclusive fingerprint evidence can be.

OK, but what has this got to do with Jesus Christ? Simply this: There is another kind of evidence that's analogous to fingerprints and establishes to an astounding degree of certainty that Jesus is indeed the Messiah of Israel and the world.

In the Jewish Scriptures, which Christians call the Old Testament, there are several dozen major prophecies about the coming of the Messiah, who would be sent by God to redeem his people. In effect, these predictions formed a figurative fingerprint that only the Anointed One would be able to match. This way, the Israelites could rule out any impostors and validate the credentials of the authentic Messiah.

The Greek word for "Messiah" is Christ. But was Jesus really the Christ? Did he miraculously fulfill these predictions that were written hundreds of years before he was born? And how do we know he was the only individual throughout history who fit the prophetic fingerprint?

There are plenty of scholars with long strings of initials after their names whom I could have asked about this topic. However, I wanted to interview someone for whom this was more than just an abstract academic exercise, and that took me to a very unlikely setting in Southern California.

INTERVIEW:
LOUIS S. LAPIDES, M.DIV., TH.M.

Usually a church would be a natural location in which to question someone about a biblical issue. But there was something different about sitting down with Pastor Louis Lapides in the sanctuary of his congregation on the morning after Sunday worship services. This setting of pews and stained glass was not where you would expect to find a nice Jewish boy from Newark, New Jersey.

Yet that's Lapides' background. For someone with his heritage, the question of whether Jesus is the long-anticipated Messiah goes beyond theory. It's intensely personal, and I had sought out Lapides so I could hear the story of his own investigation of this critical issue.

Slender and bespectacled, Lapides is soft-spoken but has a quick smile and ready laugh. He was upbeat and polite as he ushered me to a chair near the front of Beth Ariel Fellowship in Sherman Oaks, California. I didn't want to begin by debating biblical nuances; instead I started by inviting Lapides to tell me the story of his spiritual journey.

He folded his hands in his lap, looked at the dark wood walls for a moment as he decided where to start, and then began unfolding an extraordinary tale that took us from Newark to Greenwich Village to Vietnam to Los Angeles, from skepticism to faith, from Judaism to Christianity, from Jesus as irrelevant to Jesus as Messiah.

"As you know, I came from a Jewish family," he began. "I attended a conservative Jewish synagogue for seven years in preparation for bar mitzvah. Although we considered those studies to be very important, our family's faith didn't affect our everyday life very much. We didn't stop work on the Sabbath; we didn't have a kosher home."

He smiled. "However, on the High Holy Days we attended the stricter Orthodox synagogue, because somehow my dad felt that's where you went if you really wanted to get serious with God!"

When I interjected to ask what his parents had taught him about the Messiah, Lapides' answer was crisp. "It never came up," he said matter-of-factly.

I was incredulous. In fact, I thought I had misunderstood him. "You're saying it wasn't even discussed?" I asked.

"Never," he reiterated. "I don't even remember it being an issue in Hebrew school."

This was amazing to me. "How about Jesus?" I asked. "Was he ever talked about? Was his name used?"

"Only derogatorily!" Lapides quipped. "Basically, he was never discussed. My impressions of Jesus came from seeing Catholic churches: there was the cross, the crown of thorns, the pierced side, the blood coming from his head. It didn't make any sense to me. Why would you worship a man on a cross with nails in his hands and in his feet? I never once thought Jesus had any connection to the Jewish people. I just thought he was a god of the Gentiles."

I suspected that Lapides' attitudes toward Christians had gone beyond mere confusion over their beliefs. "Did you believe Christians were at the root of anti-Semitism?" I asked.

"Gentiles were looked upon as synonymous with Christians, and we were taught to be cautious because there could be anti-Semitism among the Gentiles," he said, sounding a bit diplomatic.

I pursued the issue further. "Would you say you developed some negative attitudes toward Christians?"

This time he didn't mince words. "Yes, actually I did," he said. "In fact, later when the New Testament was first presented to me, I sincerely thought it was going to basically be a handbook on anti-Semitism: how to hate Jews, how to kill Jews, how to massacre them. I thought the American Nazi Party would have been very comfortable using it as a guidebook."

I shook my head, saddened at the thought of how many other Jewish children have grown up thinking of Christians as their enemies.

A SPIRITUAL QUEST BEGINS

Lapides said several incidents dimmed his allegiance to Judaism as he was growing up. Curious about the details, I asked him to elaborate, and he immediately turned to what was clearly the most heartrending episode of his life.

"My parents got divorced when I was seventeen," he said — and surprisingly, even after all these years I could still detect hurt in his voice. "That really put a stake in any religious heart I may have had. I wondered, Where does God come in? Why didn't they go to a rabbi for counseling? What good is religion if it can't help people in a practical way? It sure couldn't keep my parents together. When they split up, part of me split as well.

"On top of that, in Judaism I didn't feel as if I had a personal relationship with God. I had a lot of beautiful ceremonies and traditions, but he was the distant and detached God of Mount Sinai who said, 'Here are the rules — you live by them, you'll be OK; I'll see you later.' And there I was, an adolescent with raging hormones, wondering, Does God relate to my struggles? Does he care about me as an individual? Well, not in any way I could see."

The divorce prompted an era of rebellion. Consumed with music and influenced by the writings of Jack Kerouac and Timothy Leary, he spent too much time in Greenwich Village coffeehouses to go to college — making him vulnerable to the draft. By 1967 he found himself on the other side of the world in a cargo boat whose volatile freight — ammunition, bombs, rockets, and other high explosives — made it a tempting target for the Vietcong.

"I remember being told at our orientation in Vietnam, 'Twenty percent of you will probably get killed, and the other eighty percent will probably get a venereal disease or become alcoholics or get hooked on drugs.' I thought, I don't even have a one percent chance of coming out normal!

"It was a very dark period. I witnessed suffering. I saw body bags; I saw the devastation from war. And I encountered anti-Semitism among some of the GIs. A few of them from the South even burned a cross one night. I probably wanted to distance myself from my Jewish identity — maybe that's why I began delving into Eastern religions."

Lapides read books on Eastern philosophies and visited Buddhist temples while in Japan. "I was extremely bothered by the evil I had seen, and I was trying to figure out how faith can deal with it," he told me. "I used to say, 'If there's a God, I don't care if I find him on Mount Sinai or Mount Fuji. I'll take him either way.' "

He survived Vietnam, returning home with a newfound taste for marijuana and plans to become a Buddhist priest. He tried to live an ascetic lifestyle of self-denial in an effort to work off the bad karma for the misdeeds of his past, but soon he realized he'd never be able to make up for all his wrongs.

Lapides was quiet for a moment. "I got depressed," he said. "I remember getting on the subway and thinking, Maybe jumping onto the tracks is the answer. I could free myself from this body and just merge with God. I was very confused. To make matters worse, I started experimenting with LSD."

Looking for a new start, he decided to move to California, where his spiritual quest continued. "I went to Buddhist meetings, but that was empty," he said. "Chinese Buddhism was atheistic, Japanese Buddhism worshiped statues of Buddha, Zen Buddhism was too elusive. I went to Scientology meetings, but they were too manipulative and controlling. Hinduism believed in all these crazy orgies that the gods would have and in gods who were blue elephants. None of it made sense; none of it was satisfying."

He even accompanied friends to meetings that had Satanic undercurrents. "I would watch and think, Something is going on here, but it's not good," he said. "In the midst of my drug-crazed world, I told my friends I believed there's a power of evil that's beyond me, that can work in me, that exists as an entity. I had seen enough evil in my life to believe that."

He looked at me with an ironic smile. "I guess I accepted Satan's existence," he said, "before I accepted God's."

"I CAN'T BELIEVE IN JESUS"

It was 1969. Lapides' curiosity prompted him to visit Sunset Strip to gawk at an evangelist who had chained himself to an eight-foot cross to protest the way local tavern owners had managed to get him evicted from his storefront ministry. There on the sidewalk Lapides encountered some Christians who engaged him in an impromptu spiritual debate.

A bit cocky, he started throwing Eastern philosophy at them. "There is no God out there," he said, gesturing toward the heavens. "We're God. I'm God. You're God. You just have to realize it."

"Well, if you're God, why don't you create a rock?" one person replied. "Just make something appear. That's what God does."

In his drug-addled mind Lapides imagined he was holding a rock. "Yeah, well, here's a rock," he said, extending his empty hand.

The Christian scoffed. "That's the difference between you and the true God," he said. "When God creates something, everyone can see it. It's objective, not subjective."

That registered with Lapides. After thinking about it for a while, he said to himself, If I find God, he's got to be objective. I'm through with this Eastern philosophy that says it's all in my mind and that I can create my own reality. God has to be an objective reality if he's going to have any meaning beyond my own imagination.

When one of the Christians brought up the name of Jesus, Lapides tried to fend him off with his stock answer. "I'm Jewish," he said. "I can't believe in Jesus."

A pastor spoke up. "Do you know of the prophecies about the Messiah?" he asked.

Lapides was taken off guard. "Prophecies?" he said. "I've never heard of them."

The minister startled Lapides by referring to some of the Old Testament predictions. Wait a minute! Lapides thought. Those are my Jewish Scriptures he's quoting! How could Jesus be in there?

When the pastor offered him a Bible, Lapides was skeptical. "Is the New Testament in there?" he asked. The pastor nodded. "OK, I'll read the Old Testament, but I'm not going to open up the other one," Lapides told him.

He was taken aback by the minister's response. "Fine," said the pastor. "Just read the Old Testament and ask the God of Abraham, Isaac, and Jacob — the God of Israel — to show you if Jesus is the Messiah. Because he is your Messiah. He came to the Jewish people initially, and then he was also the Savior of the world."

To Lapides, this was new information. Intriguing information. Astonishing information. So he went back to his apartment, opened the Old Testament to its first book, Genesis, and went hunting for Jesus among words that had been written hundreds of years before the carpenter of Nazareth had ever been born.

"PIERCED FOR OUR TRANSGRESSIONS"

"Pretty soon," Lapides told me, "I was reading the Old Testament every day and seeing one prophecy after another. For instance, Deuteronomy talked about a prophet greater than Moses who will come and whom we should listen to. I thought, Who can be greater than Moses? It sounded like the Messiah — someone as great and as respected as Moses but a greater teacher and a greater authority. I grabbed ahold of that and went searching for him."

As Lapides progressed through the Scriptures, he was stopped cold by Isaiah 53. With clarity and specificity, in a haunting prediction wrapped in exquisite poetry, here was the picture of a Messiah who would suffer and die for the sins of Israel and the world — all written more than seven hundred years before Jesus walked the earth.

He was despised and rejected by men,
a man of sorrows, and familiar with suffering.
Like one from whom men hide their faces
he was despised, and we esteemed him not.

Surely he took up our infirmities
and carried our sorrows,
yet we considered him stricken by God,
smitten by him, and afflicted.
But he was pierced for our transgressions,
he was crushed for our iniquities;
the punishment that brought us peace was upon
him,
and by his wounds we are healed.
We all, like sheep, have gone astray,
each of us has turned to his own way;
and the Lord has laid on him
the iniquity of us all.

He was oppressed and afflicted,
    yet he did not open his mouth;
he was led like a lamb to the slaughter,
    and as a sheep before her shearers is silent,
    so he did not open his mouth.
By oppression and judgment he was taken away.
    And who can speak of his descendants?
For he was cut off from the land of the living;
    for the transgression of my people he was
        stricken.
He was assigned a grave with the wicked,
    and with the rich in his death,
though he had done no violence,
    nor was any deceit in his mouth. . . .
For he bore the sin of many,
    and made intercession for the transgressors.

Isaiah 53:3 – 9, 12

Instantly Lapides recognized the portrait: this was Jesus of Nazareth! Now he was beginning to understand the paintings he had seen in the Catholic churches he had passed as a child: the suffering Jesus, the crucified Jesus, the Jesus who he now realized had been "pierced for our transgressions" as he "bore the sin of many."

As Jews in the Old Testament sought to atone for their sins through a system of animal sacrifices, here was Jesus, the ultimate sacrificial lamb of God, who paid for sin once and for all. Here was the personification of God's plan of redemption.

So breathtaking was this discovery that Lapides could only come to one conclusion: it was a fraud! He believed that Christians had rewritten the Old Testament and twisted Isaiah's words to make it sound as if the prophet had been foreshadowing Jesus.

Lapides set out to expose the deception. "I asked my stepmother to send me a Jewish Bible so I could check it out myself," he told me. "She did, and guess what? I found that it said the same thing! Now I really had to deal with it."

THE JEWISHNESS OF JESUS

Over and over Lapides would come upon prophecies in the Old Testament — more than four dozen major predictions in all. Isaiah revealed the manner of the Messiah's birth (of a virgin); Micah pinpointed the place of his birth (Bethlehem); Genesis and Jeremiah specified his ancestry (a descendent of Abraham, Isaac, and Jacob, from the tribe of Judah, the house of David); the Psalms foretold his betrayal, his

accusation by false witnesses, his manner of death
(pierced in the hands and feet, although crucifixion
hadn't been invented yet), and his resurrection (he
would not decay but would ascend on high); and on
and on.[3] Each one chipped away at Lapides' skepticism until he was finally willing to take a drastic
step.

"I decided to open the New Testament and just
read the first page," he said. "With trepidation I
slowly turned to Matthew as I looked up to heaven,
waiting for the lightning bolt to strike!"

Matthew's initial words leaped off the page: "A
record of the genealogy of Jesus Christ the son of
David, the son of Abraham . . ."

Lapides' eyes widened as he recalled the moment he first read that sentence. "I thought, Wow!
Son of Abraham, son of David — it was all fitting
together! I went to the birth narratives and thought,
Look at this! Matthew is quoting from Isaiah 7:14:
'The virgin will be with child and will give birth to
a son.' And then I saw him quoting from the prophet
Jeremiah. I sat there thinking, You know, this is
about Jewish people. Where do the Gentiles come
in? What's going on here?

"I couldn't put it down. I read through the rest of
the Gospels, and I realized this wasn't a handbook

for the American Nazi Party; it was an interaction between Jesus and the Jewish community. I got to the book of Acts and — this was incredible! — they were trying to figure out how the Jews could bring the story of Jesus to the Gentiles. Talk about role reversal!"

So convincing were the fulfilled prophecies that Lapides started telling people that he thought Jesus was the Messiah. At the time, this was merely an intellectual possibility to him, yet its implications were deeply troubling.

"I realized that if I were to accept Jesus into my life, there would have to be some significant changes in the way I was living," he explained. "I'd have to deal with the drugs, the sex, and so forth. I didn't understand that God would help me make those changes; I thought I had to clean up my life on my own."

EPIPHANY IN THE DESERT

Lapides and some friends headed into the Mojave Desert for a getaway. Spiritually he was feeling conflicted. He had been unsettled by nightmares of being torn apart by dogs pulling at him from opposite directions. Sitting among the desert scrub, he recalled the words someone had spoken to him on Sunset Strip: "You're either on God's side or on Satan's side."

He believed in the embodiment of evil — and that's not whose side he wanted to be on. So Lapides prayed, "God, I've got to come to the end of this struggle. I have to know beyond a shadow of a doubt that Jesus is the Messiah. I need to know that you, as the God of Israel, want me to believe this."

As he related the story to me, Lapides hesitated, unsure how to put into words what happened next. A few moments passed. Then he told me, "The best I can put together out of that experience is that God objectively spoke to my heart. He convinced me, experientially, that he exists. And at that point, out in the desert, in my heart I said, 'God, I accept Jesus into my life. I don't understand what I'm supposed to do with him, but I want him. I've pretty much made a mess of my life; I need you to change me.' "

And God began to do that in a process that continues to this day. "My friends knew my life had changed, and they couldn't understand it," he said. "They'd say, 'Something happened to you in the desert. You don't want to do drugs anymore. There's something different about you.'

"I would say, 'Well, I can't explain what happened. All I know is that there's someone in my life, and it's someone who's holy, who's righteous, who's a source of positive thoughts about life — and I just feel whole.' "

That last word, it seemed, said everything. "Whole," he emphasized to me, "in a way I had never felt before."

Despite the positive changes, he was concerned about breaking the news to his parents. When he finally did, reaction was mixed. "At first they were joyful because they could tell I was no longer dependent on drugs and I sounded much better emotionally," he recalled. "But that began to unravel when they understood the source of all the changes. They winced, as if to say, 'Why does it have to be Jesus? Why can't it be something else?' They didn't know what to do with it."

With a trace of sadness in his voice, he added, "I'm still not sure they really do."

Through a remarkable string of circumstances, Lapides' prayer for a wife was answered when he met Deborah, who was also Jewish and a follower of Jesus. She took him to her church — the same one, it turned out, that was pastored by the minister who many months earlier on Sunset Strip had challenged Lapides to read the Old Testament.

Lapides laughed. "I'll tell you what — his jaw dropped open when he saw me walk into the church!"

That congregation was filled with ex-bikers, ex-hippies, and ex-addicts from the Strip, along with a spattering of transplanted Southerners. For a young Jewish man from Newark who was relationally gun-shy with people who were different from him, because of the anti-Semitism he feared he would encounter, it was healing to learn to call such a diverse crowd "brothers and sisters."

Lapides married Deborah a year after they met. Since then she has given birth to two sons. And together they've given birth to Beth Ariel Fellowship, a home for Jews and Gentiles who also are finding wholeness in Christ.

RESPONDING TO OBJECTIONS

Lapides finished his story and relaxed in his chair. I let the moment linger. The sanctuary was peaceful; the stained glass was glowing red and yellow and blue from the California sun. I sat musing over the power of one person's story of a faith found. I marveled at this saga of war and drugs, of Greenwich Village and Sunset Strip and a barren desert, none of which I ever would have associated with the pleasant, well-adjusted minister sitting in front of me.

But I didn't want to ignore the obvious questions that his story raised. With Lapides' permission I started by asking the one that was foremost on my mind: "If the prophecies were so obvious to you and pointed so unquestionably toward Jesus, why don't more Jews accept him as their Messiah?"

It was a question Lapides has asked himself a lot during the three decades since he was challenged by a Christian to investigate the Jewish Scriptures. "In my case, I took the time to read them," he replied. "Oddly enough, even though the Jewish people are known for having high intellects, in this area there's a lot of ignorance.

"Plus you have countermissionary organizations that hold seminars in synagogues to try to disprove the messianic prophecies. Jewish people hear them and use them as an excuse for not exploring the prophecies personally. They'll say, 'The rabbi told me there's nothing to this.'

"I'll ask them, 'Do you think the rabbi just brought up an objection that Christianity has never heard before? I mean, scholars have been working on this for hundreds of years! There's great literature out there and powerful Christian answers to those challenges.' If they're interested, I help them go further."

I wondered about the ostracism a Jewish person faces if he or she becomes a Christian. "That's definitely a factor," he said. "Some people won't let the messianic prophecies grab them, because they're afraid of the repercussions — potential rejection by their family and the Jewish community. That's not easy to face. Believe me, I know."

Even so, some of the challenges to the prophecies sound pretty convincing when a person first hears them. So one by one I posed the most common objections to Lapides to see how he would respond.

1. The Coincidence Argument

First, I asked Lapides whether it's possible that Jesus merely fulfilled the prophecies by accident. Maybe he's just one of many throughout history who have coincidentally fit the prophetic fingerprint.

"Not a chance," came his response. "The odds are so astronomical that they rule that out. Someone did the math and figured out that the probability of just eight prophecies being fulfilled is one chance in one hundred million billion. That number is millions of times greater than the total number of people who've ever walked the planet!

"He calculated that if you took this number of silver dollars, they would cover the state of Texas to a depth of two feet. If you marked one silver dollar among them and then had a blindfolded person wander the whole state and bend down to pick up one coin, what would be the odds he'd choose the one that had been marked?"

With that he answered his own question: "The same odds that anybody in history could have fulfilled just eight of the prophecies."

I had studied this same statistical analysis by mathematician Peter W. Stoner when I was investigating the messianic prophecies for myself. Stoner also computed that the probability of fulfilling forty-eight prophecies was one chance in a trillion, trillion, trillion, trillion, trillion, trillion, trillion, trillion, trillion, trillion, trillion, trillion, trillion![4]

Our minds can't comprehend a number that big. This is a staggering statistic that's equal to the number of minuscule atoms in a trillion, trillion, trillion, trillion, billion universes the size of our universe!

"The odds alone say it would be impossible for anyone to fulfill the Old Testament prophecies,"

Lapides concluded. "Yet Jesus — and only Jesus throughout all of history — managed to do it."

The words of the apostle Peter popped into my head: "But the things which God announced beforehand by the mouth of all the prophets, that His Christ should suffer, He has thus fulfilled" (Acts 3:18 NASB).

2. The Altered Gospel Argument

I painted another scenario for Lapides, asking, "Isn't it possible that the gospel writers fabricated details to make it appear that Jesus fulfilled the prophecies?

"For example," I said, "the prophecies say the Messiah's bones would remain unbroken, so maybe John invented the story about the Romans breaking the legs of the two thieves being crucified with Jesus, and not breaking his legs. And the prophecies talk about betrayal for thirty pieces of silver, so maybe Matthew played fast and loose with the facts and said, yeah, Judas sold out Jesus for that same amount."

But that objection didn't fly any further than the previous one. "In God's wisdom, he created checks and balances both inside and outside the Christian community," Lapides explained. "When the gospels were being circulated, there were people living who had been around when all these things happened. Someone would have said to Matthew, 'You know it didn't happen that way. We're trying to communicate a life of righteousness and truth, so don't taint it with a lie.' "

Besides, he added, why would Matthew have fabricated fulfilled prophecies and then willingly allowed himself to be put to death for following someone who he secretly knew was really not the Messiah? That wouldn't make any sense.

What's more, the Jewish community would have jumped on any opportunity to discredit the Gospels by pointing out falsehoods. "They would have said, 'I was there, and Jesus' bones were broken by the Romans during the Crucifixion,' " Lapides said. "But even though the Jewish Talmud refers to Jesus in derogatory ways, it never once makes the claim that the fulfillment of prophecies was falsified. Not one time."

3. The Intentional Fulfillment Argument

Some skeptics have asserted that Jesus merely maneuvered his life in a way to fulfill the prophecies. "Couldn't he have read in Zechariah that the Messiah would ride a donkey into Jerusalem, and then arrange to do exactly that?" I asked.

Lapides made a small concession. "For a few of the prophecies, yes, that's certainly conceivable," he said. "But there are many others for which this just wouldn't have been possible.

"For instance, how would he control the fact that the Sanhedrin offered Judas thirty pieces of silver to betray him? How could he arrange for his ancestry, or the place of his birth, or his method of execution, or that soldiers gambled for his clothing, or that his legs remained unbroken on the cross? How would he arrange to perform miracles in front of skeptics? How would he arrange for his resurrection? And how would he arrange to be born when he was?"

That last comment piqued my curiosity. "What do you mean by when he was born?" I asked.

"When you interpret Daniel 9:24 – 26, it foretells that the Messiah would appear a certain length of time after King Artaxerxes I issued a decree for the Jewish people to go from Persia to rebuild the walls in Jerusalem," Lapides replied.

He leaned forward to deliver the clincher: "That puts the anticipated appearance of the Messiah at the exact moment in history when Jesus showed up," he said. "Certainly that's nothing he could have prearranged."[5]

4. *The Context Argument*

One other objection needed to be addressed: were the passages that Christians identify as messianic prophecies really intended to point to the coming of the Anointed One, or do Christians rip them out of context and misinterpret them?

Lapides sighed. "You know, I go through the books that people write to try to tear down what we believe. That's not fun to do, but I spend the time to look at each objection individually and then to research the context and the wording in the original language," he said. "And every single time, the prophecies have stood up and shown themselves to be true.

"So here's my challenge to skeptics: don't accept my word for it, but don't accept your rabbi's either. Spend the time to research it yourself. Today nobody can say, 'There's no information.' There are plenty of books out there to help you.

"And one more thing: sincerely ask God to show you whether or not Jesus is the Messiah. That's what I did — and without any coaching it became clear to me who fit the fingerprint of the Messiah."

CONCLUSION

THE VERDICT
OF HISTORY

What Does the Evidence Establish — And What Does It Mean Today?

WAS JESUS REALLY CONVINCED THAT HE WAS THE SON OF GOD?

By going back to the very earliest traditions, which are unquestionably safe from legendary development, Ben Witherington III was able to show that Jesus had a supreme and transcendent self-understanding. Based on the evidence, Witherington said, "Did Jesus believe he was the Son of God, the anointed one of God? The answer is yes. Did he see himself as the Son of Man? The answer is yes. Did he see himself as the final Messiah? Yes, that's the way he viewed himself. Did he believe that anybody less than God could save the world? No, I don't believe he did."

DID JESUS — AND JESUS ALONE — MATCH THE IDENTITY OF THE MESSIAH?

Hundreds of years before Jesus was born, prophets foretold the coming of the Messiah, or the Anointed One, who would redeem God's people. In effect, dozens of these Old Testament prophecies created a fingerprint that only the true Messiah could fit. This gave Israel a way to rule out impostors and validate the credentials of the authentic Messiah. Against astronomical odds — one chance in a trillion, trillion, trillion, trillion, trillion, trillion, trillion, trillion, trillion, trillion, trillion, trillion, trillion — Jesus, and only Jesus throughout history, matched this prophetic fingerprint. This confirms Jesus' identity to an incredible degree of certainty.

REACHING YOUR OWN VERDICT

So what about you? You've heard some of my experience, but your own conclusion is up to you. No one can make up your mind for you.

Maybe, after exploring some of the issues and evidence, you've decided, as I did, that the case for Christ is conclusive. What's next? If you want to ex-

perience Christ for yourself, all you need is to receive Jesus' grace. You can do that by talking to him
from your heart, admitting the things you've done
wrong, and accepting Jesus as your forgiver and
leader. You'll become his son or daughter, and you'll
be launched on a spiritual adventure that will con-
tinue for the rest of your life — and into eternity.

But maybe you still have questions. Then keep
searching. One of the best things you can do is to
read the Bible for yourself. (You might like to try *The
Journey*, which is an edition of the Bible for people
who aren't yet sure that it's the word of God.)

You might even think about asking God for help.
After all, what's to lose? If nobody's really there in
heaven, all you've lost is a few seconds. But if God
is real and he is listening — well, you could be a
winner in a big way.

Here's the prayer I prayed when I started my own
investigation into the case for Christ:

> God, I don't even believe you're there, but if
> you are, I want to find you. I really do want
> to know the truth. So if you exist, please
> show yourself to me.

You can use this or one of your own. But brace
yourself: You may get what you ask for. I did.

NOTES

CHAPTER 1: THE IDENTITY EVIDENCE

1. Marjorie Rosen, "Getting Inside the Mind of a Serial Killer," *Biography* (October 1997), 62 – 65.

2. Ibid., 64.

CHAPTER 2: THE FINGERPRINT EVIDENCE

1. Evans, *The Casebook of Forensic Detection*, 98 – 100.

2. Lee Strobel, " 'Textbook' Thumbprint Aids Conviction in Coed's Killing," *Chicago Tribune* (June 29, 1976).

3. For basic details on fulfilled prophecies, see McDowell, *Evidence That Demands a Verdict*, 141 – 77.

4. Peter W. Stoner, *Science Speaks* (Chicago: Moody Press, 1969), 109.

5. For a discussion of the Daniel prophecy, see Robert C. Newman, "Fulfilled Prophecy As Miracle," in R. Douglas Geivett and Gary R. Habermas, eds., *In Defense of Miracles* (Downers Grove, Ill.: InterVarsity Press, 1997), 214 – 25.

WILLOW
Willow Creek Association

Willow Creek Association
Vision, Training, Resources for Prevailing Churches

This resource was created to serve you and to help you build a local church that prevails. It is just one of many ministry tools that are part of the Willow Creek Resources® line, published by the Willow Creek Association together with Zondervan.

The Willow Creek Association (WCA) was created in 1992 to serve a rapidly growing number of churches from across the denominational spectrum that are committed to helping unchurched people become fully devoted followers of Christ. Membership in the WCA now numbers over 12,000 Member Churches worldwide from more than ninety denominations.

The Willow Creek Association links like-minded Christian leaders with each other and with strategic vision, training, and resources in order to help them build prevailing churches designed to reach their redemptive potential. Here are some of the ways the WCA does that.

- **The Leadership Summit**—a once a year, two-and-a-half-day conference to envision and equip Christians with leadership gifts and responsibilities. Presented live at Willow Creek as well as via satellite broadcast to over 130 locations across North America, this event is designed to increase the leadership effectiveness of pastors, ministry staff, volunteer church leaders, and Christians in the marketplace.

- **Ministry-Specific Conferences** — throughout each year the WCA hosts a variety of conferences and training events — both at Willow Creek's main campus and offsite, across the U.S., and around the world — targeting church leaders and volunteers in ministry-specific areas such as: small groups, preaching and teaching, the arts, children, students, volunteers, stewardship, etc.

- **Willow Creek Resources®** — provides churches with trusted and field-tested ministry resources in such areas as leadership, evangelism, spiritual formation, spiritual gifts, small groups, stewardship, student ministry, children's ministry, the use of the arts — drama, media, contemporary music — and more.

- **WCA Member Benefits** — includes substantial discounts to WCA training events, a 20 percent discount on all Willow Creek Resources®, *Defining Moments* monthly audio journal for leaders, quarterly *Willow* magazine, access to a Members-Only section on WillowNet, monthly communications, and more. Member Churches also receive special discounts and premier services through WCA's growing number of ministry partners — Select Service Providers — and save an average of $500 annually depending on the level of engagement.

For specific information about WCA conferences, resources, membership, and other ministry services contact:

Willow Creek Association
P.O. Box 3188
Barrington, IL 60011-3188
Phone: 847-570-9812
Fax: 847-765-5046
www.willowcreek.com

The complete title, The Case for Christ, includes an investigation of many additional topics

The Case for Christ

A Journalist's Personal Investigation of the Evidence for Jesus

Is Jesus really the divine Son of God? What reason is there to believe that he is?

In his bestseller *The Case for Christ*, the legally trained investigative reporter Lee Strobel examined the claims of Christ by retracing his own spiritual journey, reaching the hard-won yet satisfying verdict that Jesus is God's unique son.

Written in the style of a blockbuster investigative report, *The Case for Christ* consults a dozen authorities on Jesus with doctorates from Cambridge, Princeton, Brandeis, and other top-flight institutions to present:

- Historical evidence
- Scientific evidence
- Psychiatric evidence
- Fingerprint evidence
- Other evidence

This colorful, hard-hitting book is no novel. It's a riveting quest for the truth about history's most compelling figure.

Hardcover 0-310-22646-5   Unabridged Audio CD 0-310-24779-9
Softcover 0-310-20930-7

We want to hear from you. Please send
your comments about this book to us in care of
zreview@zondervan.com. Thank you.